70 FABULOUS THINGS TO MAKE WITH

PAPERCRAFTS

70 FABULOUS THINGS TO MAKE WITH
PAPERCRAFTS

Sensational step-by-step projects for cards, gift wraps, papier-mâché,
crafts and creative stationery with over 400 fabulous photographs

MARION ELLIOT & ANGELA A'COURT

southwater

This edition is published by Southwater

Southwater is an imprint of Anness Publishing Ltd
Hermes House, 88–89 Blackfriars Road, London SE1 8HA
tel. 020 7401 2077; fax 020 7633 9499
www.southwaterbooks.com; info@anness.com

© Anness Publishing Ltd 2006

UK agent: The Manning Partnership Ltd
6 The Old Dairy, Melcombe Road, Bath BA2 3LR
tel. 01225 478444; fax 01225 478440
sales@manning-partnership.co.uk

UK distributor: Grantham Book Services Ltd, Isaac Newton Way
Alma Park Industrial Estate, Grantham, Lincs NG31 9SD
tel. 01476 541080; fax 01476 541061; orders@gbs.tbs-ltd.co.uk

North American agent/distributor: National Book Network
4501 Forbes Boulevard, Suite 200, Lanham, MD 20706
tel. 301 459 3366; fax 301 429 5746; www.nbnbooks.com

Australian agent/distributor: Pan Macmillan Australia
Level 18, St Martins Tower, 31 Market St, Sydney, NSW 2000
tel. 1300 135 113; fax 1300 135 103; customer.service@macmillan.com.au

New Zealand agent/distributor: David Bateman Ltd
30 Tarndale Grove, Off Bush Road, Albany, Auckland
tel. (09) 415 7664; fax (09) 415 8892

Publisher: Joanna Lorenz
Editorial Director: Judith Simons
Editors: Penelope Cream and Elizabeth Woodland
Art Director: Peter Bridgewater
Designer: Michael Morey
Cover Designer: Balley Design Associates
Photographer: Martin Morris
Illustrator: Lorraine Harrison
Production Controller: Pedro Nelson

Previously published as part of a larger volume, *The Art and Craft of Paper*

10 9 8 7 6 5 4 3 2 1

PUBLISHER'S NOTE
No occupation is gentler than papercraft, but some general points
should be remembered for safety and care of the environment.

▮ Always choose non-toxic materials whenever possible: for example,
PVA strong clear glue, non-toxic varnishes and poster paints.

▮ Craft knives, scissors and all cutting implements should be used
with care. Children love papercrafts, but should only be allowed to
use sharp tools under supervision.

▮ Always use a cutting board or cutting mat to avoid damage to
household surfaces (it is also safer to cut onto a firm, hard surface).

▮ Protect surfaces from paint, glue and varnish splashes by laying
down old newspapers.

Main front cover image shows Gift Bag, see page 44; and a greeting card
variation of Decorative Doily, see page 81.

Contents

Introduction

Paper is everywhere: our lives would be impossible without wrappings, letters, magazines, cards, packaging, leaflets, posters, newspapers and notepads. It is one of the most inexpensive and readily available of materials, yet it is commonly neglected as a craft, art and hobby medium. With know-how, imagination and enthusiasm, papercraft skills and papier-mâché artistry can transform this simple, functional and cost-effective material into fantastic gifts, wonderful shapes, delightful stationery and beautiful objects, such as toys, bags, jewellery and boxes.

Decorative Stationery, Cards and Envelopes

Everyone enjoys receiving hand-made greetings cards and letters,
and the ones in this section are eye-catching and fun to make.
There are some wonderful ideas to try out, including making
your own paper, stencilled patterns and striking batik effects.
There are also more unusual projects for stationery, such as
Tiger Stripes and Hopping Frogs, and creative designs for cards,
including a delightful pop-up Valentine's Heart, as well as
Practical and Elegant Envelopes.

PAPER-MAKING

Paper-making is an ancient art form, practised for many centuries since the process was first discovered by the Chinese. It can be very satisfying to make your own paper. If you want to make paper of writing quality, dissolve two teaspoons of size powder in a pint of warm water and add it to your pulp. It is possible to produce many interesting effects in your paper. Small pieces of coloured paper can be added to the pulp to give a speckled effect; this can also be achieved by adding organic material such as tea leaves, seeds, hair, leaves and flower petals. It is also possible to colour and perfume your paper by adding waterproof ink or a few drops of scent to the pulp.

YOU WILL NEED
Waste paper
Blender or liquidizer
Fine sieve
Rectangular bowl
Kitchen cloths (one for each piece of
*   paper to be made) or towelling*
Newspaper
Paper-making frame (deckle and
*   mould)*
Two wooden boards

MAKING PULP

To make paper pulp, tear up waste paper into small pieces. The lighter the colour of waste paper used, the paler the result; newspaper will produce a greyish paper. Old computer printout paper is good. Place the torn paper in a bucket of warm water and let it soak overnight. To reduce the paper to a pulp, squeeze out as much water as possible, and place a small handful of the mushy paper into a blender or liquidizer, covering it with two parts of water. Blend the paper and water together for a few seconds at a time. Add more water if the pulp is too thick for the blender to rotate freely.

1 When you have pulped all the soaked paper, drain it through a fine sieve, and place three or four handfuls in the rectangular bowl. Cover the pulp with warm water. You will need roughly three parts of water to one part pulp.
  Before you start to make your paper, prepare a 'couching mound'. This is a small pile of wet material such as kitchen cloths or towelling, cut or folded to the same size as the frame and placed on top of a thick wedge of newspaper. The pulp is transferred from the mould onto this mound to dry.

2 Take your paper-making frame. The mesh-covered frame is called the mould, and the open frame is the deckle. Position the mould mesh-side up, and place the deckle on top of it.

3 Put the frame into the far end of the bowl, with the deckle facing you.

4 Next, submerge the frame in the pulp.

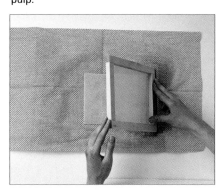

5 Pull the frame gently towards you, while holding on to keep it tightly closed and completely submerged. Lift the frame from the bowl, keeping it horizontal. Let the frame rest on the side of the bowl for a minute to drain, and then remove the deckle.

6 Stand the mould on its short side and lower it onto the couching mound, pressing it down firmly. Then lift the bottom edge off the couching cloth, and remove the frame. The pulp will stick to the cloth. Cover the pulp with an opened-out kitchen cloth, and continue couching sheets of paper, covering each new piece with another kitchen cloth.

7 When you have used all the pulp, or feel that you have made enough paper, cover the last piece with a kitchen cloth, and transfer the pile of cloths containing your paper on its couching mound and pile of newspaper onto one of the wooden boards. The board should be placed on a surface that is easy to mop

dry as a great deal of water will come out of the paper.

Place the second board on top of the pile, and then stand or lean heavily on it to press the paper flat. Press on the paper for a couple of minutes.

Remove the pile of cloths from the newspaper, then gently lift the top cloth, uncovering

the last piece of paper that you made, and lay it out, still on its cloth, on a flat surface to dry. Do the same with every piece of paper. The sheets may take two days to dry properly. To remove the paper from its drying cloth, slip a blunt knife under its edge and gently separate the two.

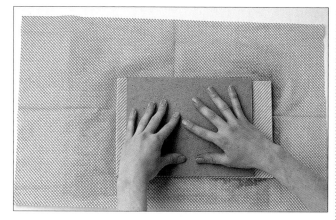

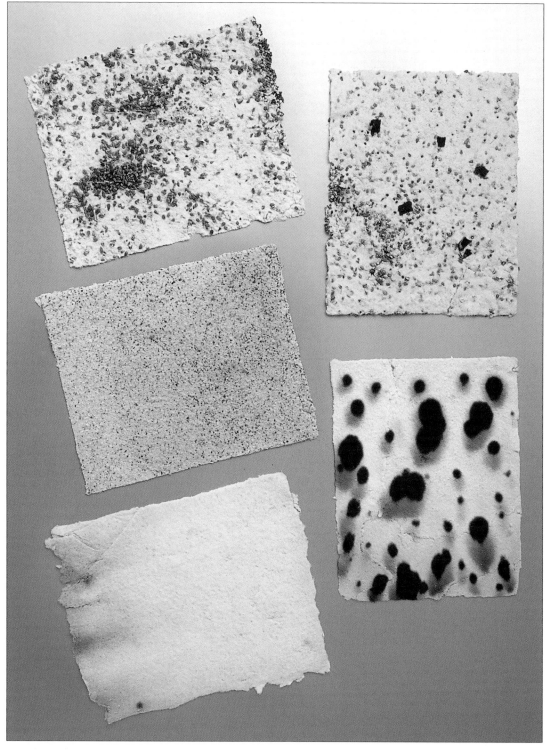

ABSTRACT STATIONERY

Every piece of writing paper will be different using this technique of tearing and gluing paper to create an abstract design.

YOU WILL NEED
Craft knife
Writing paper
Card (stock) in two contrasting colours
Glue

1 Using a craft knife, cut a small rectangle at the top of the writing paper, in the centre. Next, choose two pieces of different colour card just large enough to cover the opening, and tear one in half.

2 Glue one of the torn halves onto the other whole rectangle.

3 Glue this onto the back of the letterhead.

4 Instead of using a plain card, a favourite patterned wrapping paper can be put behind the opening. Different shaped openings can be cut for the effect you like. In this step some paper is glued on to card and then slotted in and glued so that it breaks up the top line of the paper.

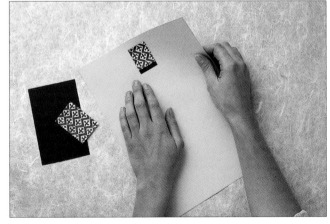

5 Of course the plain and patterned papers can be mixed.

STENCILLED PAPER

Stencilling is a very popular craft and a huge variety of effects can be achieved. Stencilled patterns can be combined with other decorative techniques such as speckling or batik effects using wax crayons. Either a stencilling brush or a sponge can be used to apply the paint through the stencil; a brush will give a stippled effect, and a sponge a solid, denser result.

YOU WILL NEED
Stencilling card
Craft knife
Paper
Assortment of paints
Piece of sponge
Stencil brush

1 Draw a design onto the stencilling card and cut it out carefully using a craft knife.

2 Lay a piece of paper onto a flat surface and place the stencil on top over the intended position of the design. Mix the paint until it is quite sticky in consistency; take up a fair amount of paint using the sponge and carefully dab it over the pattern in the stencilling card. Take care not to let the paint become too thin as it will seep under the edges of the stencil, giving a blurred design.

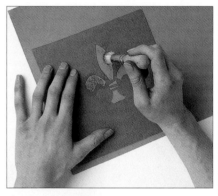

3 To use a stencil brush, lay a sheet of paper down on a flat surface and place the stencil on top. Load the brush with fairly thick paint and press it gently over the stencil, covering the paper beneath. Again, make sure the paint is not too thin. Dab paint over the stencil so that a mottled effect is achieved.

STENCIL STYLE

Use ready-made or cut your own stencils to make this stylish writing paper. Dab on stencil paints or colour with soft crayons for speedy results.

YOU WILL NEED
Stencilling card
Craft knife
Paint
Stencil brush
Writing paper
Crayon

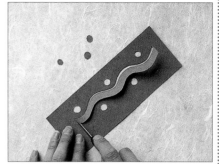

1 Using the template transfer the motif onto stencilling card in the size you require and cut out using a craft knife.

2 Prepare the paint on a saucer and collect the colour onto a stencil brush. Then, holding the stencilling card firmly with one hand, use the other to dab the brush onto the writing paper using a circular movement.

3 Instead of using paint, a coloured crayon could be used. Once again hold the stencilling card firmly in one hand and lightly fill in the pattern, remembering to work the crayon strokes in the same direction each time.

BATIK
EFFECTS

Lovely batik-like effects can be
achieved on paper with wax crayons
and thin paint. Designers' inks, which
have very intense colours, can be used
for striking results. Leave a central
space clear of wax for writing on.

YOU WILL NEED
White and coloured paper
Wax crayons
*Assorted poster or gouache paints, or
    designers' inks*
Clear wax candle

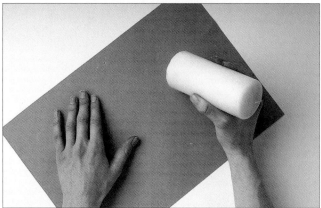

1 Draw a design
onto white paper
with wax crayons,
using either a single
colour or a variety.
Load a paint brush
with thin paint or
diluted ink and
brush it over the
wax. Two coats of
paint can be applied
to achieve a stronger
colour layer where
required.

2 To create a multi-
coloured effect
where the base
colour of the paper
will show through,
use a clear wax
candle to draw the
design onto
coloured paper.
Paint over the wax
marks with one
colour and leave to
dry. Next, make
more wax marks and
paint over the paper
again with a second
colour so that the
second set of designs
will take on the
colour of the first
layer of paint.

CLASSIC
LINES

If you want to write a letter in a hurry, but still want it to be stylish, here are a couple of quick ways to make some beautiful writing paper. You will need some lightly coloured wrapping paper in a classical design.

YOU WILL NEED
Pale wrapping paper
Tracing paper
Glue
Sheet of white paper

1 Cut out a rectangle of wrapping paper to the size of writing paper, and cut a piece of tracing paper to the same size. Stick the tracing paper on top of the wrapping paper, smoothing out any bubbles. Use a black felt-tip pen to write your letter so that it shows up clearly.

2 If you have a bit more time you could select one particular motif from the paper and cut this out.

3 Glue the motif to a sheet of white paper.

4 As before, glue a sheet of tracing paper on top to give an elegant double layer. You could make a collection of writing paper by cutting out different motifs from one sheet of wrapping paper.

CUT-OUT STATIONERY

A fleur-de-lys motif is used for this writing paper cut-out, but you could choose a simple heart shape or your initial as decoration.

YOU WILL NEED
Plain writing paper
Craft knife
Contrasting coloured paper
Glue

1 Scale the motif from the template up or down to the required size or design your own and transfer it onto the centre of the top of the writing paper.

2 Carefully cut out the background area with a craft knife. Using a pair of scissors cut out a small rectangle of a different coloured card just larger than the motif.

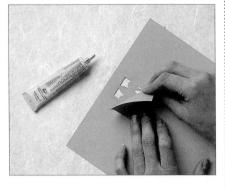

3 Turn the writing paper over, glue around the opening and then stick down the contrasting coloured card. Turn the paper back again and see how the motif stands out.

TIGER STRIPES AND HOPPING FROGS

Here are some ideas for making writing paper with an animal theme. You can use these ideas to design original writing paper, based on your favourite animal.

YOU WILL NEED
Orange, black, blue and green paper
Glue
Writing paper

3 For a fishy theme cut out shapes of watery ripples and a swimming fish from blue paper and then stick them at the top and bottom of the page.

4 This hopping frog theme is made by cutting out a frog shape in green paper and fixing it to the top of the page.

You will then need to cut out and glue small squares of green paper to represent its hop!

1 To make a jungle theme take a piece of orange paper and cut out 'stripy' shapes from a piece of black paper.

2 Arrange the tiger stripes down one side of the paper and glue them into position.
To add colour to a sheet of white writing paper you can also cut out an abstract squiggle and glue it onto the right hand side.

CUT-AND-THREAD PAPER

Make plain writing paper extra special with simple strips of crêpe paper threaded through in unusual patterns. Practise first on spare paper to get the right effect.

YOU WILL NEED
Sheet of writing paper
Craft knife
Crêpe paper

1 Take a sheet of writing paper and mark two sets of two vertical lines at the top, in the centre. The lines should be approximately 2 cm (¾ in) long and 2½ cm (1 in) apart. Cut through the lines using a craft knife.

2 Cut a piece of crêpe paper in a toning colour to your writing paper. Thread it under the 'bridges' taking care not to break them.

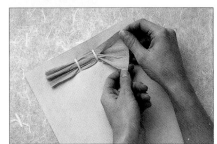

3 Once the crêpe paper is centred arrange the bow by fanning out the sides.

4 Repeat the bow design on the extended back flap of an envelope to complete the writing set.

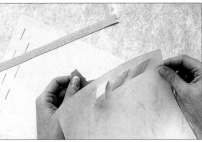

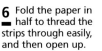

5 Another effect can be achieved by marking and cutting out a series of vertical lines across the top of the page. Cut a piece of crêpe paper the same width as the slots, and a thinner strip in a stronger colour.

6 Fold the paper in half to thread the strips through easily, and then open up.

7 Instead of using vertical lines this version uses two staggered lines of horizontal slits. Once again thread the strip of crêpe paper through and see the diagonal pattern it makes.

VALENTINE'S HEART

This pop-up surprise will add a touch of fun to Valentine's Day. The same technique can be used to make cards for other occasions, such as a tree for Christmas time, or a house for a friend's moving day.

YOU WILL NEED
Stiff paper in two different colours
Glue

1 Scale up the support from the template to the required size and cut out of a piece of stiff paper. Then fold a matching piece of paper into two halves to form a card. Fold the support to the correct shape, creasing the tabs upwards.

8 cm
(3½ in)

7 cm
(3 in)

Support

2 Next, glue the support to the backing card near the top, ensuring that the crease on the support exactly touches the crease on the card. Note that the support is symmetrically placed over the crease.

3 Cut out a heart shape in red paper and glue it to the tabs at the top of the support. Decorate the inside border of the card to match. When the card is opened the heart will spring out and surprise the recipient!

BROWN PAPER STATIONERY

Sometimes you need very little to make a good impression. For this project recycled brown paper is used to decorate the sheets of writing paper.

YOU WILL NEED
Brown paper
Plain writing paper
Glue
Gold metallic pen
Black felt-tip pen

1 For the first idea, tear a thin strip of the brown paper and glue it down, either on the right-hand side of the page or across the top as illustrated.

2 Then take a gold pen and draw a design along the strip. Remember that you can invent your own designs.

3 As an alternative suggestion, stick down pieces of brown paper to make two corner strips. Take the gold pen, draw in a design and then give it a three-dimensional effect by outlining it in a black felt-tip pen.

4 Another variation on the same theme is to tear a wider strip of brown paper and then tear it into four squares. Glue these down at the top of the paper and then decorate with black spots using a felt-tip pen.

ACROSS THE BORDER

By making the back half of this card slightly wider than the front it enables you to decorate the created border in many ways.

YOU WILL NEED
*Assorted coloured paper or
    card (stock)*
Silver metallic pen
Glue
Felt-tip pens
Tissue paper

5 This version is slightly more complicated. Take a piece of bright card and fold into the basic shape, then glue a panel of contrasting wrapping paper onto the front. When it is fixed, trim at the sides and then draw an arch and bauble design onto the leading edge. Cut out the arch and bauble shape.

1 To make the basic card fold a rectangle in two so that the top side is slightly shorter than the back.

2 Now shape the front fold by cutting a zigzag border.

3 Stick a contrasting coloured card behind to make the serrated edge stand out.

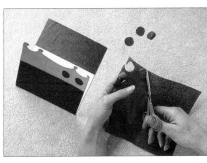

4 Alternatively, cut out a wavy edge on the front side and then decorate it with a silver line following the curved line. To finish the decoration draw a row of whirls.

6 On the inside of the card glue down a panel of contrasting tissue paper.

7 Cut further small circles in the tissue paper and glue them along the border.

FLOWER POWER

A simple idea for a get well or Mother's Day card. As an alternative, choose yellow backing paper for a birthday design.

YOU WILL NEED
Thin card (stock) in three colours
Craft knife
Glue

1 Take a rectangle of card and fold it in half. Draw the 'daisy' pattern onto one half of the card and with the card opened out flat cut out the shapes using a craft knife.

2 Cut a piece of pink card to the same size as the folded card. On the inside of the main card spread glue around the cut-out areas and place over the pink card.

3 Cut out orange circles from the remaining card and glue in place to make the centres of the daisies.

24

TEARING HURRY

Using pieces of torn paper to create an abstract design, these cards are unusual and unique! Experiment with colours and cards for the best effect.

YOU WILL NEED
Envelope
Card (stock)
Ruler
Craft knife
Paper scraps
Glue

1 Using the size of an envelope as a guide, cut out a piece of complementary card three times as wide. Divide and mark the card into three equal parts. In the central panel cut out an opening with a ruler and a craft knife to create the frame.

2 Tear up pieces of paper into similarly-sized, irregular shapes and start to arrange them on the left hand panel.

3 Once you are happy with the arrangement of the collage pieces they can be glued into position. Complete the card by gluing around the frame in the centre panel and sticking it down over the artwork. Fold the blank sheet round to form the card shape and add your message.

For this style of card it is best to have a tall image so that the majority of the folded card remains intact and is able to stand up. A palm tree card is described here, but you could use similar techniques to create the architectural variations shown.

YOU WILL NEED
Assorted coloured card (stock)
Orange and brown
*   paper*
Glue

1 Take a square of coloured card and fold in half. Draw out the shape of the palm tree leaves on the front and cut out the uppermost ones through both layers.

2 Then cut out coconuts from orange and brown paper and stick them onto the card at the base of the leaves.

3 Draw a tree trunk shape on light green card and cut out. Cut a zigzag edge along one side and glue this onto the card.

ENVELOPE LETTERS

There is no need for an envelope if you make this clever stationery that folds up like a notelet. Seal it with a sequin and pop it in the post.

YOU WILL NEED
Sheet of writing paper
Glue
Sequin
Double-sided tape

1 Fold a sheet of writing paper into three parts so that the top third is slightly smaller than the others.

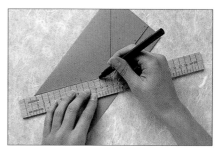

2 On the top fold draw a line from the centre to each corner to make an envelope flap and then cut off the corner triangles.

3 To decorate the top, glue a sequin at the point. A piece of gold, metallic or shiny card would work as well.

4 Just under the flap attach a small piece of double-sided sticky tape and then draw in address lines on the reverse.

5 There are lots of different ways to decorate the envelope letter. You can glue on strips of contrasting coloured paper so that when the paper is folded up it looks like a present.

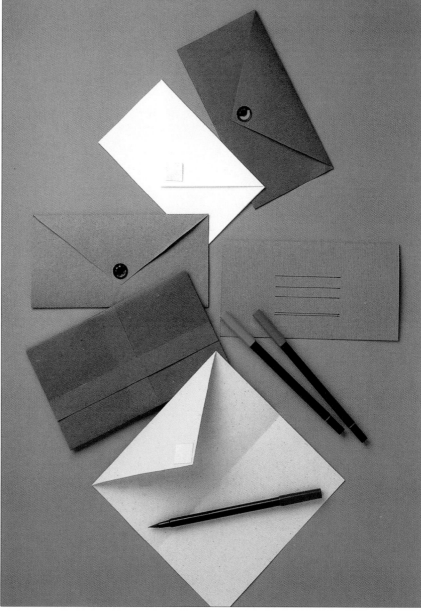

PRACTICAL ENVELOPE

Home-made envelopes can be cheaper and a lot more fun than shop-bought ones. Make a set from a variety of different papers, both plain and patterned. In order to write the address on a patterned paper simply add a little white label.

YOU WILL NEED
Stiff paper
Glue

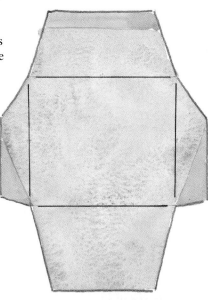

1 Scale up the template to the size required and transfer to the stiff paper. Using a scissor blade, gently score along the back of the creases that are to be folded. Next, fold in the side flaps.

2 Glue the bottom flap to the side flaps to form the envelope. Pop in your letter or card, seal with a dab of glue and send it off!

ELEGANT ENVELOPES

Finding the right size and style of envelope to match your home-made stationery can be a problem, so why not make your own?

YOU WILL NEED
Coloured card (stock)
Glue
Contrasting coloured card (stock)

1 Measure out the size that you require by placing your card onto a piece of coloured card. It must be twice as long plus 3 cm (1 in), and as wide plus 6 cm (2 in). For a pointed flap you will need an extra 10 cm (4 in) on the length.

2 Cut off the excess corners and then fold up the bottom and sides and stick them down.

3 Cut out a motif to stick on the back flap in a different colour. If the envelope has a pointed flap you might like to make this a contrasting colour by cutting out a triangle to the same size and gluing it to the back flap.

NOTELET HOLDER

Take an ordinary writing pad and envelopes and dress them up in a special notelet holder. All kinds of versions are possible, made from decorative papers and cards.

YOU WILL NEED
Writing paper and envelopes
Card (stock)
Glue
Brown paper or wrapping paper
Gold metallic pen
String
2 paper fasteners

1 To make the notelet holder use one of the envelopes to determine the size, and cut a piece of card, measuring the length of the envelope and adding 8 cm (3 in), by three times the height of the envelope plus 8 cm (3 in).

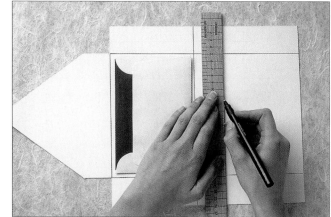

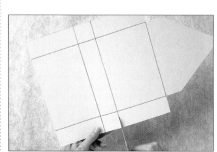

2 Cut out the card with or without the pointed flap according to the finished style that you require.

3 Apply glue to the unmarked side of the cut out card, and then cover in brown paper, trimming the edges where necessary. In this example the paper covering is decorated by hand, but you could use a favourite wrapping paper or a piece of wallpaper.

4 Taking a gold pen draw a design onto the brown paper.

5 On the inside, score along the marked lines and cut the tab lines.

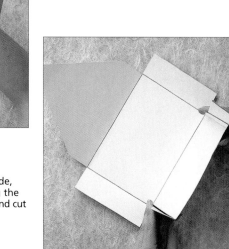

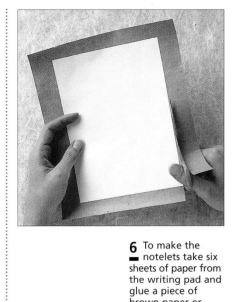

7 Decorate the brown paper with the gold pen as before. Fold the paper in half and pop the six notelets and envelopes into the notelet holder.

6 To make the notelets take six sheets of paper from the writing pad and glue a piece of brown paper or wrapping paper onto each sheet of writing paper. Trim to size.

8 Now fold and glue the notelet holder together. To make the closure push the fasteners through the paper at the point of envelope flap and in the front of the box to one side of the flap. Secure the case with a loop of string round the fasteners.

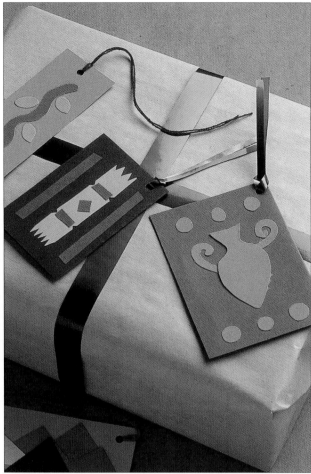

Gift Wrap,
Boxes
and Tags

The projects in this chapter will show you how to add a touch of elegance to any present, and the best thing about them is that they are all easy to make. There are imaginative ideas for creating your own gift wrap designs, such as block printing and sponging, or simply by using contrasting paints. There are designs for sophisticated gift boxes, such as a Curvy-edged Box and a Confectionery Box, which make charming hiding places for keepsakes. You will also find projects for decorative ribbons and rosettes, as well as tips for creating fun gift tags.

BLOCK PRINTING

Printing is a great way to cover sheets of wrapping paper with a uniform pattern, and you can use the blocks to make matching stationery too. Try stars or Christmas trees for a festive paper.

YOU WILL NEED
Potatoes
Craft knife
Erasers
Poster or gouache paints
Ink pad
Paper
Nail brush
Stiff cardboard

1 To make a potato block, first cut the potato in half, making sure that the cut surface is straight and flat so that the design will print evenly onto the paper. The design can be cut directly into the potato, or else it can be drawn first with a pencil and then carefully pared away using a craft knife. Use the same process to make blocks from erasers.

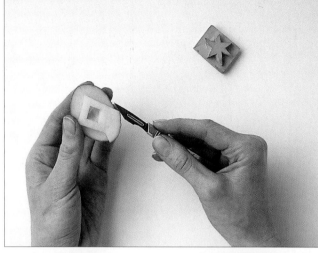

2 Mix the paint with a little water and dab it onto the surface of the block with a paint brush.

Firmly press the block onto a piece of paper and lift it up again, taking care to use a direct upwards movement to avoid smudging the printed image.

3 Rubber blocks can be used with ink pads as well as with paint.

4 Block printing can be combined with speckling in contrasting colours to create a very lively effect. Here, purple paper with a black block design is speckled using a nail brush dipped in yellow paint. Hold the brush over the paper and draw a piece of stiff cardboard over the bristles, making sure the cardboard is pulled towards the body (to avoid splashing yourself with paint!).

5 Cut a set of symbols into some erasers and use them on letter-heads and envelopes for a personalized look to your stationery.

SPECKLING EFFECTS

Speckling produces a variety of results depending on how the paint is applied, and on how sharply the brush is shaken. Gentle taps produce fine marks, rather like freckles. More boisterous movements can produce a more startling effect.

YOU WILL NEED
A selection of papers
Assorted poster or gouache paints
Length of wood or other object to tap brush against
Nail brush
Stiff cardboard

1 Lay the sheet of paper to be speckled on a flat surface. Mix the paint to a fairly thin consistency and load a paint brush with it. Hold the length of wood over the paper and bring the brush down on the wood, tapping along its length over the paper to produce a speckled effect.

2 More than one colour of speckling can be applied; colours that tone in with the first layer of paint or even those which contrast sharply with it can look very effective. To obtain a fine spray of speckles dip a nail brush in thin paint and position it over the paper, holding it with the bristles uppermost. Pull a strip of cardboard over the bristles (taking care to pull it *towards* your body so that you do not splash yourself with paint), moving the brush around the paper to create an even coating of paint.

DECORATIVE SPONGING

Sponging has been used as a form of decoration for many years, especially on pottery. The process gives a pleasing mottled effect to plain surfaces, and can be very bold and dramatic; or, if you prefer, a more subtle background pattern can also be obtained.

YOU WILL NEED
Selection of poster or gouache paints
Piece of natural sponge
Paper
Newspaper

1 Mix a little paint in a saucer or on a small palette. The paint should be fairly sticky. Dip the sponge into the paint and dab it lightly over the surface of the paper, making a random pattern. If you want to be certain of the thickness of the pattern, test the density of the paint first by dabbing the sponge on newspaper.

2 To create patterns with two or more colours, wash the sponge thoroughly and squeeze it almost dry. When the first layer of sponging has dried, add more colours one by one, making sure each has time to dry before the next coat.

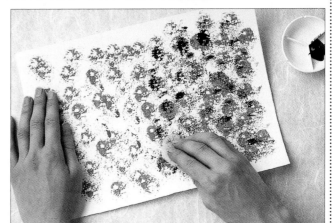

ANTIQUE MARBLING

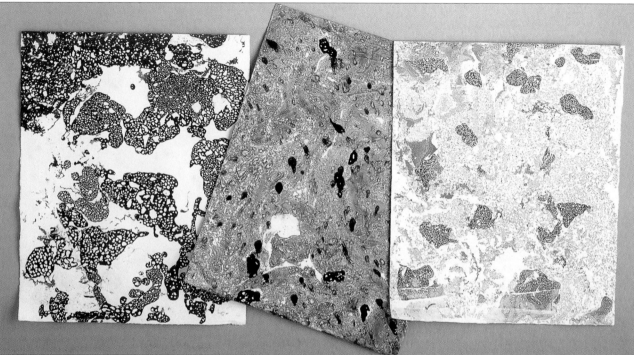

There are several methods of marbling paper to achieve the beautiful effects seen on old bookbinding and traditional Italian stationery. The process involves suspending pigment on top of water, arranging the colour into patterns, and transferring these to paper.

YOU WILL NEED
Metal roasting pan or deep tray
Paper
Oil paints in various colours
White spirit
Paint brush or metal skewer

1 Half fill a clean metal roasting pan or a deep tray with cold water. Cut a piece of paper to fit the size of the tray. Thin a little oil paint with white spirit, and dot the diluted paint onto the surface of the water with a brush.

2 The paint will disperse, creating patterns on the surface of the water. Hold the paper by the top right- and bottom left-hand corners and lower it across the surface of the water in a rolling movement.

3 Carefully lift the paper from the tray. The paint will adhere to the paper, giving a marbled effect. Lay the sheets out to dry at room temperature.

4 To create multi-coloured patterns add two or more colours of oil paint to the surface of the water. Use the end of a paint brush or a metal skewer to move the colours around before laying the paper down on the water. Before marbling subsequent pieces of paper, skim the surface of the water with scrap paper to pick up excess paint and keep the water clean.

PAINT AND PAPER

Have fun turning an ordinary piece of black paper into bright and jazzy wrapping paper. You could of course vary the colour of the paper and paints.

YOU WILL NEED
Plain paper
Paints

2 Add more colours as you wish until the paper is brightly decorated.

1 Take a piece of black paper large enough to cover your present. Now choose the paint colours you are going to use. This example uses fuchsia pink, orange and gold paints to contrast with the black background. After preparing the paint on a saucer, decorate the paper with random 'blobs', working with one colour at a time.

3 For a more regular painted pattern, the present can be wrapped first and then, following the shape of the gift, painted with wavy lines.

TWO-TONE GIFT WRAP

Here is another way to make your own wrapping paper, this time using two layers of co-ordinating crêpe paper.

YOU WILL NEED
Crêpe paper in two contrasting colours
Glue

1 First work out how much paper you will need in order to cover the gift. Now cut a piece of paper to this size in each of your two chosen colours. Decide which colour will be on top and pleat it lengthwise.

2 Now cut circles out through all the layers along both sides of the pleat.

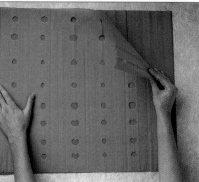

3 Open up the top paper and glue it onto the bottom. It is exciting to see how the colour of the bottom layer shows through. If you want a really elaborate design, add cut-out pieces in a further colour, leaving openings large enough to reveal the colours beneath. Now wrap your gift up in the two-tone dotty paper.

BOW-TIE GIFT WRAP

Here is an interesting way to present your gifts by making your own three-dimensional bow-tie wrapping paper.

YOU WILL NEED
Crêpe paper in two or three contrasting colours
Double-sided tape or glue

1 First wrap your gift in a plain crêpe paper. To make the bows, cut out 5 cm (2 in) wide strips of contrasting crêpe paper and then cut them into 6 cm (2½ in) lengths.

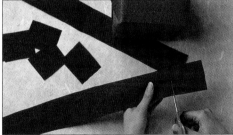

2 Gather each piece in the middle and then twist to make the bow shape.

3 Now attach the bows to the wrapped gift either with double-sided tape or some glue.

4 To make your present really stand out, make up the bows in two different colours twisted together.

WRAPPING A ROUND OBJECT

A round present is always a difficult shape to wrap up and it can be approached in two ways. The gift can either be placed in the centre of a piece of paper which can then be gathered up into a bunch above the present and tied with ribbon, or the paper can be pleated, as here.

YOU WILL NEED
Wrapping paper
Sticky tape
Double-sided tape

1 Place the present in the centre of a square piece of paper. Make the square into a circle by rounding off the corners.

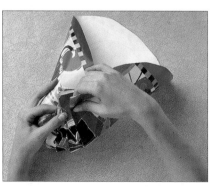

2 Start by bringing one section of the paper up to the top. Now work around the circle by pleating the paper so that it hugs the shape of the sphere. Use tape to secure the pleats as you go round.

3 Continue to pleat neatly until you have gone all the way around. To finish off the top, make a pleated fan. Take a long strip of paper and fold in half with the right side outside. Pleat the paper along its length.

4 Then, pinch the pleats together at the bottom and fan out the sides. Attach it to the present by fixing with double-sided tape.

DECORATIVE WALLET

Make this tidy wallet out of a favourite colour paper or piece of wrapping paper. You could even design the pattern yourself. This simple wallet is perfect for putting smaller gifts in.

YOU WILL NEED
Stiff paper or wrapping paper
Craft knife
Glue

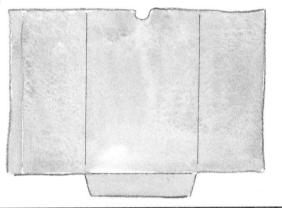

1 Scale up the template to the size required and transfer the pattern onto the paper. Cut around the edges using a craft knife. Fold the sides inwards and glue one long edge to the other.

2 Glue the bottom flap to seal the end of the wallet, and it is ready for use.

GIFT BAG

This gift bag is simple to make and adds a touch of elegance to any present. It can be used instead of separate wrapping paper and is sturdy enough to hold a variety of gifts.

YOU WILL NEED
Decorated paper
Craft knife
Glue
Hole punch
Ribbon

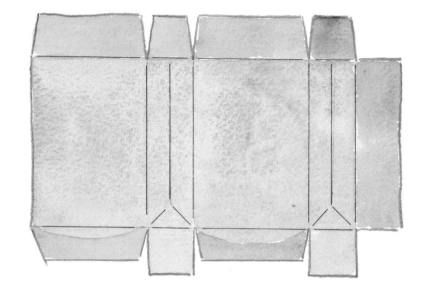

1 Scale up the template to the size required and transfer the pattern onto the decorated paper. Cut out carefully using a craft knife. Score lightly along the back of the creases so that they will fold more easily. Fold down and glue the flaps along the *top* edge of the bag.

2 Next, glue the long, side tab to form the bag shape.

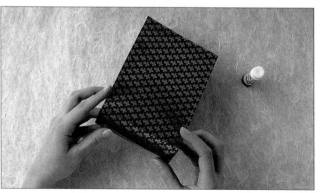

3 Then glue the base of the bag, folding in the short end tabs first.

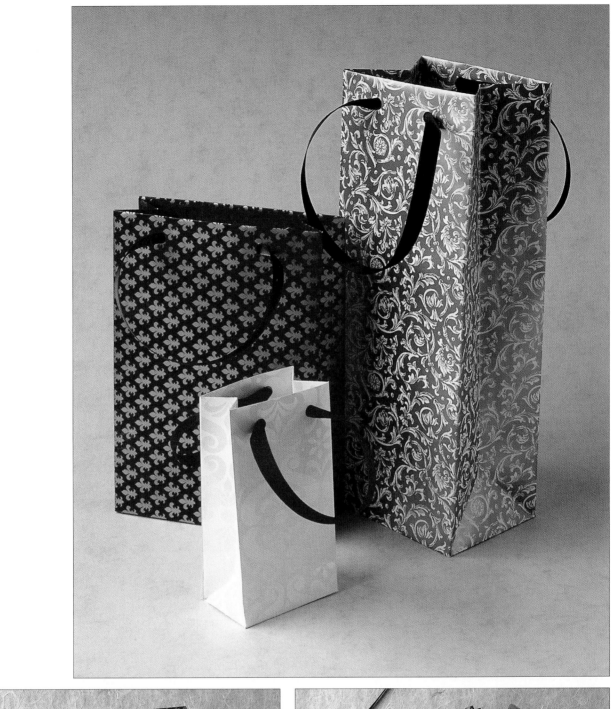

4 Form the pleats down the sides of the bag by pressing the long edges together gently so that the paper is pushed inwards.

5 Using the hole punch, make two holes on each of the top sides near the upper edge. Cut two short lengths of ribbon and thread each end through the holes to make two looped handles. Knot the ends at the back of the holes to secure.

GIFT BOX

Here is an easy and stylish way to present an awkwardly-shaped gift. It also makes a lovely box to use afterwards to keep things in.

YOU WILL NEED
Empty shoe box with lid
Patterned and plain wrapping paper
Glue
Tissue paper

1 Wrap the outside of the box in the patterned paper.

2 Now line the inside of the box with plain paper.

3 Cover the lid of the box on the top and inside in the plain paper. Take some tissue paper in a co-ordinating colour, softly scrunch it up and arrange it in the bottom of the box. Place the gift inside and put the lid on.

4 As a further decoration, enhance the top by attaching paper strips cut from the patterned paper to suggest ribbons.

CURVY-EDGED BOX

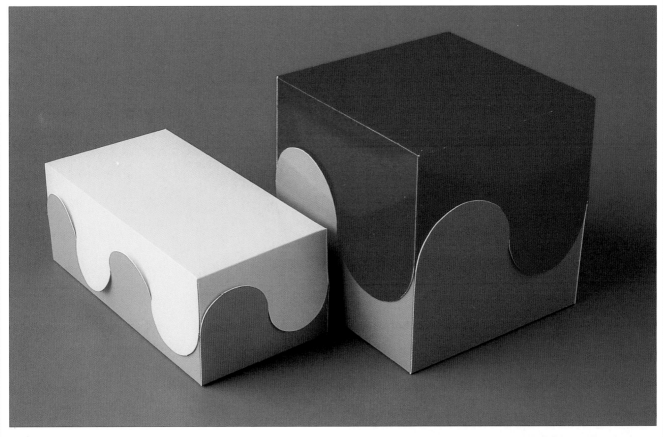

This unusual box is almost as pretty in two halves as it is when assembled. To get the maximum effect choose two contrasting or complementary colours for the two halves so that the pattern of the curves stands out.

YOU WILL NEED
Thin card (stock) in two different
  colours
Craft knife
Glue

1 Scale up the template to the size required and transfer the pattern twice to a piece of card, once for each half of the box. Cut out the patterns using a craft knife, taking extra care around the curves. Both halves are made in the same way: fold and glue each tab beneath the semi-circles to form the sides.

2 Repeat the process with the other half, gluing each side firmly.

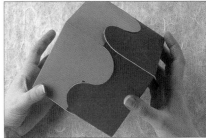

3 To assemble the box, interlock the two halves, making sure each semi-circle overlaps on the outside of the box.

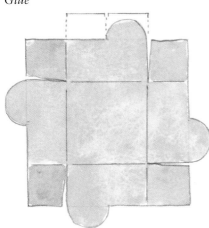

ONE-PIECE
GIFT BOXES

This box is constructed from a single piece of card and can be closed tightly, making it an ideal container, either vertical or horizontal, for home-made edible gifts, such as small cakes.

YOU WILL NEED
Thin card (stock)
Craft knife
Glue

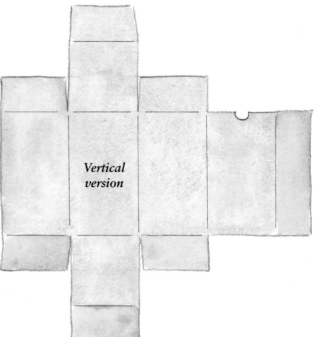

Vertical version

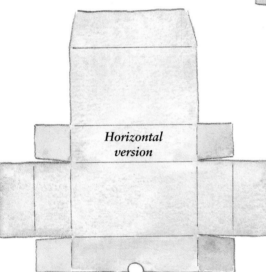

Horizontal version

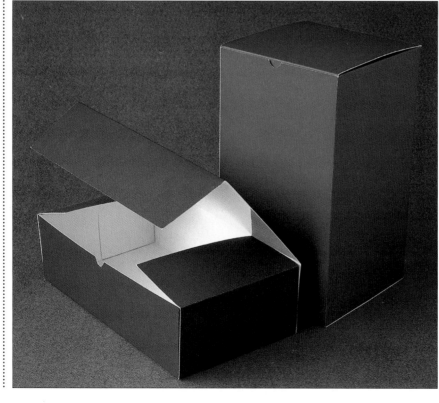

1 Scale up the template to the size required, and transfer it to the card. Cut it out using a craft knife. Score along the back folds of the tabs. Fold up the sides of the box and glue the end tab to make a tube shape.

2 Interlock the tabs at the base of the box and the base should lock securely without glue.

CONFECTIONERY BOX

This box is quick and easy to assemble.
It needs only a spot of glue and a few
tucks. Fill it with chocolates or
home-made truffles for the perfect gift.

YOU WILL NEED
Thin coloured card (stock)
Craft knife
Glue

1 First, scale up the
pattern from the
template to the size
required and
transfer to the piece
of card. Cut out
using a craft knife,
scoring along the
back of the creases.
Glue the end tab to
form the basic box
shape.

2 Next, interlock
the tabs at the
base of the box. If
the pattern has been
carefully cut out, the
base will lock
strongly without
glue. Fill the box
with chocolates and
fold down the lid.

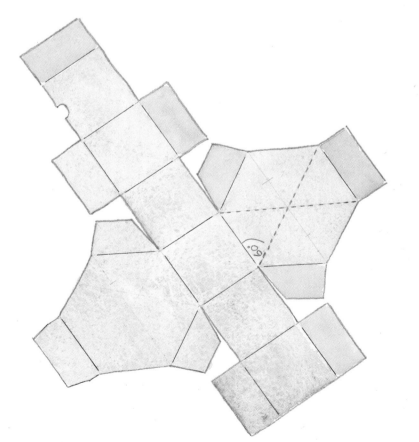

RIBBON BRAIDS AND CURLS

There are many different effects that can be achieved by mixing and matching coloured ribbons. They can be braided or twisted and grouped into colours to cascade down a wrapped present.

YOU WILL NEED
Assortment of ribbons
Double-sided tape
Felt-tip pens
Gold metallic pen

1 One of the most straightforward ways to use ribbon is to curl it. This effect is achieved by pulling the ribbon through closed scissors to make it twist and fall into natural ringlets. Try doing this to different lengths and colours of ribbons and then attach a bunch of curls to your present.

2 Another effective way to use ribbon is to braid it, using at least three different colours. Tape the ribbon ends together and braid to the required length. Secure and cut the ribbon ends.

3 In this example a whole medley of ribbons in different colours and widths is put together in order to create a riot of colour. Tape and cut ribbon ends.

4 To give ribbon an individual look, decorate it by drawing a design taken from the wrapping paper with a felt-tip or metallic pen.

GIFT WRAP, BOXES AND TAGS

RIBBON ROSETTES

Make gifts look extra special with ribbon rosettes that match your wrapping paper. There are many ways of making ribbons into rosettes, pompoms or just simple bows. Choose from all the types of plain and fancy ribbons available, or make your own by cutting strips from the wrapping paper.

YOU WILL NEED
Ribbon
Double-sided tape

1 Cut eight lengths of ribbon, four 30 cm (12 in) long and the other four measuring 24 cm (9 in). Make each one into a loop by using double-sided tape.

2 Assemble the rosette by crossing two of the longer loops and taping them in the middle. Then make another cross and join to the first cross, making the bottom layer.

3 Repeat with the shorter loops and join these to the base.

4 Finish off by putting a small loop into the centre and fixing it onto your wrapped gift.

5 To make a different ribbon trim, grade the loops to start with a 30 cm (12 in) loop and make each layer smaller by 5 cm (2 in). Holding the loops in the middle, glue them one on top of the other, starting with the largest at the bottom and getting smaller to form a fan shape.

TAG TIME

Make your own gift tags for a personal touch as well as to save money. Used greetings cards can often be cut down and made into brand new gift tags. Another idea is to take a motif from the wrapping paper used to cover your present.

YOU WILL NEED
Wrapping paper or greetings cards
Glue
Thin card (stock)
Ribbon

1 When you have wrapped the present, cut out a suitable motif from the spare paper. Glue the motif onto some thin card in a co-ordinating colour.

2 Following the shape of the motif cut around the design so that the card forms a border.

3 Now punch a hole in the card with a scissor blade and thread a ribbon through the hole. Write a message on the tag and attach it to the present.

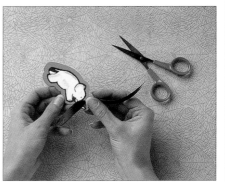

COLLAGE TAGS

When you want to keep things simple
and have perhaps used a plain paper
to wrap your present, a collaged gift
tag can be the perfect finishing touch.
They can be as easy or as complicated
as you want to make them.

YOU WILL NEED
Orange card (stock)
Green paper
Glue
Coloured thread

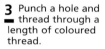

1 For the Grecian-
style tag cut out a
Grecian urn and
decorative dots in
green paper.

2 Glue them onto a
folded piece of
orange card.

3 Punch a hole and
thread through a
length of coloured
thread.

FRUIT 'N' VEG

Here is a fruity number that makes a collection of fun gift tags. These are just a few ideas from the wide variety of interesting shapes that can be found in fruit, vegetables and flowers, such as peas, bananas and sunflowers.

YOU WILL NEED
Orange, green and yellow card (stock)
Sticky tape
Coloured felt-tip pens

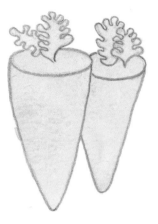

1 For a carrot gift tag scale up the template and transfer to the orange card. Cut out the pair of carrots, making sure that the top is not cut in order to leave the fold intact. Now cut out some greenery.

2 Open out the card and cut two slots with a craft knife at the top of the carrots.

3 Next, push the greenery through the slots and secure on the back with some tape.

4 The last stage is to draw the shading marks onto the carrot with a brown felt-tip pen.

SECRET MESSAGES

Give a sense of mystery to your gifts by adding a tag tied with a ribbon bow to conceal your message. A perfect idea for sending notes to loved ones.

YOU WILL NEED
Coloured card (stock)
Contrasting coloured paper
Gold metallic pen
Glue
Ribbon

1 Take a rectangle of card and fold in half. Open out the card and make a small narrow slit for the ribbon on the centre of both leading edges, back and front.

2 On a separate piece of black paper draw a design with a gold pen and stick this onto the card.

3 Write your message inside and then thread a length of gold ribbon through the slits and tie a bow to keep the wording a secret.

Decorative Ornaments and Gifts

In this chapter there is a fabulous collection of fun projects
to make. You will find simple paper toys with movable
limbs – Cut-out Animals and a Performing Pierrot – as well
as a pendant to hang in your window, which looks like
stained glass. There are also papier-mâché projects,
including a decorative bowl and a Spotty Dog. All these
projects will inspire adults and children alike, and they make
great gifts for friends and family too.

BAROQUE BAUBLES

We have used a polystyrene ball for this decoration. They can be bought, in a range of sizes, from craft suppliers and are used for making dolls' heads.

YOU WILL NEED
Polystyrene (Styrofoam) ball
Gouache paint
Gold doily
Glue
Brass paper fastener
Gold thread

1 First of all, paint the bauble with some gouache in a suitable colour.

2 When the paint has dried, cut out pieces from a doily. Decide how they are to be arranged on the bauble and glue them into position.

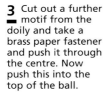

3 Cut out a further motif from the doily and take a brass paper fastener and push it through the centre. Now push this into the top of the ball.

4 Taking some gold thread, wrap it around the brass fastener so that it is ready to be hung on the Christmas tree.

ORIENTAL FAN

Here is an easy way to make a beautiful fan to cool yourself on a hot summer's day. This fan is loosely based on a Japanese fan and so we have made it with Japanese rice paper.

YOU WILL NEED
Thin card (stock)
Craft knife
Glue
Double-sided tape
Rice paper or tissue paper

1 Cut out an oval piece of thin card. Make sure that the card is not too thick so that it is flexible for fanning. Cut out the bottom area of the fan with a craft knife.

2 Next cut thin strips of card and lining them up at the base, stick them on both sides of the fan so that they follow the cut out lines.

3 To make the handle, cut out two strips of thicker card measuring 14 × 1½ cm (5½ × ½ in). Taper the ends and stick double-sided tape onto both pieces. Attach them to either side of the base part of the fan.

4 Now cover the fan in rice paper by gluing round the edge and along the struts. We have used a different colour paper on either side for variety. If you cannot find rice paper, use tissue paper instead. Trim the edges with scissors.

5 Cover the handle by wrapping it with a long strip of rice paper and gluing it at the bottom.

CONCENTRIC TWIST

Hang this impressive paper sculpture in a window; if it is made from metallic-coated card it will catch the light as it moves gently in the air currents.

YOU WILL NEED
Thin coloured card (stock)
Craft knife

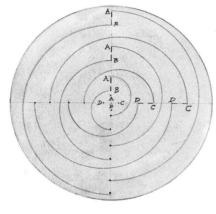

1 Scale up the template to the required size and transfer to coloured card. Cut the slits using a craft knife. Gently twist the outer circle away from its frame.

2 Starting at the rim, form the first twist again by gently turning the central section at an angle of 90 degrees to the outer ring.

3 Continue to form the twists by turning each ring at the same angle, moving progressively towards the centre, until the twist-out is complete.

CUT-OUT ANIMALS

The chicken, frog and elephant are held together with paper fasteners and have moveable limbs. They are very simple in construction, and many other animals could be attempted using the same process.

YOU WILL NEED
Heavy paper or thin card (stock)
Felt-tip pens or coloured pencils
Craft knife
Paper fasteners
Glue

1 Scale up your chosen animal from the template to the required size, and transfer the pieces to paper or card. Cut two bodies for each animal. Remember that one will have to be cut *in reverse* so that the bodies can be stuck together. Next, cut two of each leg, wing, ear and so on. To transfer the pattern in reverse, simply turn it over.

2 Next, colour each piece of animal with felt-tip pen or coloured pencils, and cut them all out, keeping the parts separate.

3 To fix the animal together, make a small incision with a craft knife at the limb positions in each body, and at the top of each body part. Push a paper fastener through the front of each body part, through the body, and open it out on the other side to secure the animal.

4 To join the two halves together, spread a little glue along the top edge of one half of the animal's body, and stick it to the other.

PERFORMING PIERROT

Children will love to watch the clever movements of this traditional Pierrot puppet. Why not make a couple and put on a show?

YOU WILL NEED
Blue, white and red paper
Black felt-tip pen
Glue
4 paper fasteners
Metal skewer or scissor blade
Curtain ring
Thin string

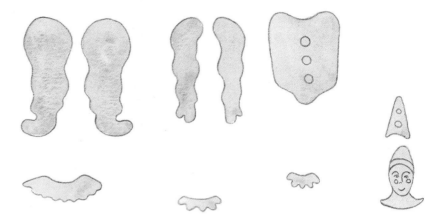

1 Scale up the pieces from the template to the size required and transfer to the coloured paper. Cut out the shapes for the clown: one body, two legs, two arms and a hat in blue, collar, cuffs and pom-poms in white. Mark on reference dots with a black pen. First make up the face by gluing on his hat and rosy cheeks. Draw the face details in with a black felt-tip pen.

2 Glue the pom-poms onto the hat, front and Pierrot's boots, and stick on the collar and cuffs.

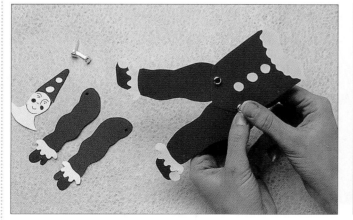

3 Match up the dots on the body and limbs and join them all together by pushing the paper fasteners through both layers. Open out the fasteners on the back.

4 On the reverse side, pull the limbs downwards and pierce a hole at the top of each arm using a skewer or scissor blade. Thread a length of thin string through each hole and knot at both ends, on the reverse side. Repeat this with the legs to form two 'cross bars'.

DECORATIVE ORNAMENTS AND GIFTS

5 Thread a long piece of string through a curtain ring. Attach one end to the centre of the arm string and the other end to the centre of the leg string. Trim where necessary. The strings should not be slack when the limbs are 'at rest'. When the strings are firmly fixed, pull the ring and watch Pierrot perform.

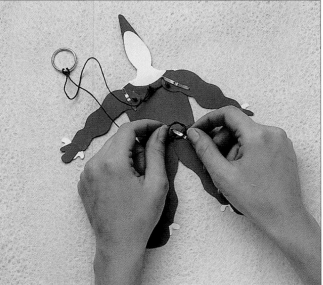

SPOTTY DOG

This spotty dog is made from tightly rolled and twisted newspaper. It is a very good method for the construction of other animals, giving a firm armature or support for papier-mâché. It might be fun to make a giraffe or an elephant to go into a papier-mâché ark!

YOU WILL NEED

Newspaper
Masking tape
Diluted PVA (white) glue
Fine sandpaper
White paint
Assortment of poster paints
Non-toxic clear gloss varnish

1 Take two double spread sheets of newspaper and twist them tightly to form a 'rope'. Tape the ends of the rope, and then bend it to form a fat rectangle about 15 cm (6 in) long, with one end extending about 5 cm (2 in). This end will form the dog's head. Firmly tape the rectangle to hold it in place.

2 Make the dog's limbs in the same way as the body and head. Using a single sheet of newspaper, form a thinner 'rope', and tape it along its length. Cut it into four pieces about 7–10 cm (3–4 in) long, and fix each one in place on the dog's body using masking tape. Add the dog's ears and tail with small, thin rolls of paper.

3 Soak newspaper strips in diluted PVA glue and cover the dog with three layers of papier-mâché strips. Leave it to dry overnight in a warm place.

4 Sand down the papier-mâché dog shape, and prime it with two coats of white paint. Decorate the dog with poster paints, and then seal with two coats of clear gloss varnish.

DOLL

This doll is formed from tightly taped and compacted newspaper twists. The resulting structure is very sturdy and quite large dolls or other toys could be constructed using this method.

YOU WILL NEED
Newspaper
Masking tape
Diluted PVA (white) glue
Fine sandpaper
White paint
Selection of poster paints
Black ink (optional)
Non-toxic clear gloss varnish

1 First, twist a double sheet of newspaper together to form a 'rope' and tape the top, about 5 cm (2 in) down, to form the doll's head. Cut the remaining paper 'rope' to the desired length to form the body, and secure it with masking tape.

2 Cover the body and head with strips of masking tape to add extra strength. Next, make the arms and legs by the same process, twisting smaller pieces of paper and taping them along their length. Cut the resulting 'ropes' to the right length, and tape them firmly in place on the doll's body.

3 Tear some newspaper into thin strips and soak in diluted PVA glue. Then cover the doll with four layers of papier-mâché. To make the doll's hair, hands and feet, roll up small strips of glue-soaked paper between finger and thumb to form pellets of pulp and stick them in place on the head. Paper over the pulp hair with short, thin strips of paper.

4 Let the doll dry overnight in a warm place. When completely dry, lightly smooth the surface with fine sandpaper and prime it with two coats of white paint.

5 When the paint has dried thoroughly, draw in the features of the doll with pencil and fill in the design with poster paints. Define the decoration with black ink if more detail is needed. Seal the doll with two coats of non-toxic clear gloss varnish and allow to dry.

■ PAINTED VASE

This vase is not waterproof, but it can be used to hold artificial or dried flowers, and is a very decorative 'objet d'art' in its own right. It is made using a simple basic method that can be easily adapted to make other shapes or sizes of vase.

YOU WILL NEED
Heavy corrugated cardboard
Strong clear glue
Masking tape
Newspaper
Diluted PVA (white) glue
Fine sandpaper
White paint
Assorted poster paints
Non-toxic clear gloss varnish

*Front/
back*

*Cut
2*

*Wall
of
vase*

1 Scale up the shapes from the template to the size required and transfer onto heavy corrugated cardboard and cut out. The vase wall should be placed on the cardboard so that the corrugations run across the wall's width. This will make it easier to bend the wall into

shape. Glue and tape the wall into place right around the inside edge of one of the vase pieces. Cover the pieces with a coat of diluted PVA glue to help prevent warping, and let them dry for three to four hours in a warm place.

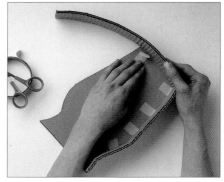

2 Next, tear narrow strips of newspaper and soak in diluted PVA glue. Cover the pieces of vase with four layers of papier-mâché strips. Leave to dry flat in a warm place overnight, and then smooth them lightly with fine sandpaper. Cover the inside of the vase and wall, and the remaining vase piece with two coats of white paint.

3 Join the vase together, with the painted surfaces to the inside. Glue the pieces together with strong clear glue and tape over the join with masking tape.

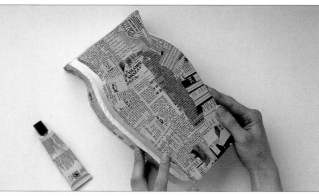

4 Leave the vase to dry for at least an hour. When dry seal its joined edge with three layers of papier-mâché strips, taking care to ensure a smooth surface by pushing out any small air bubbles or excess glue.

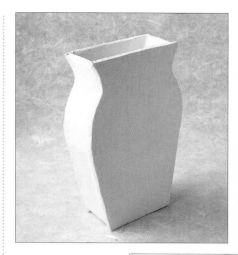

6 To decorate, lightly draw on the design with a pencil and then fill in using poster paints. When the paint is completely dry, apply a coat of clear gloss varnish.

5 Let the vase dry overnight, sand it lightly, and prime with two coats of white paint.

POPULAR POPPIES

The stark simplicity of bright red poppies with their black centres makes them an ideal flower to craft in paper.

YOU WILL NEED
Garden wire
Cotton wool (cotton balls)
Green, black and red crêpe paper
Glue
Sticky tape

1 To make the stem cut a length of garden wire. Bend the top to make a loop and trap a small amount of cotton wool in the loop. Cover this in a cut-out circle of green crêpe paper. Secure by wrapping tape around.

2 Next cut three small circles of black crêpe paper. Fringe the outer edges and then poke the other end of the wire through the centre and slide up to the green bud.

3 Cut out five petal shapes in red crêpe paper and stretch the outer edge with your finger tips so that they frill.

4 Glue the petals one by one around the base of the centre.

5 Finally, cover the stem in green crêpe paper by winding a long strip around diagonally and securing it at the base with sticky tape.

BANGLES AND BEADS

If you want some new accessories and to wear something that nobody else will have, this jewellery that is made from paper could be just what you are looking for.

YOU WILL NEED

Patterned paper
Contrasting coloured card (stock)
Pencil or paint brush
Glue
Bead thread
Sticky tape

1 To start, cut 30 cm (12 in) strips of marbled or decorated paper and taper them so that they measure 4 cm (1½ in) at the base and 1 cm (½ in) at the tip. Then cut a small length of contrasting coloured card, wrap it around a pencil or paint brush and fix it with glue.

3 To make a matching bangle, cut a long strip of white card and curl it round into a ring, large enough to slip over your hand. Fix by taping it.

2 Now apply some more glue to the length of the triangular strip and, beginning with the wider end, start to wrap around the card, so that the strip is kept central. Make several more of these beads, and thread them onto a length of bead thread to form a necklace.

4 Now cut long strips of your chosen decorated paper and after gluing them at one end, start to wind them one by one around the bangle shape.

BOWLED OVER

This bowl is made by a traditional method where layers of papier-mâché are laid into a greased mould and removed when dry. For this project, an ordinary china bowl has been used, but all sorts of items can make interesting moulds – just remember to grease them first, otherwise they will be permanently lined with paper!

YOU WILL NEED
Bowl suitable for using as a mould
Petroleum jelly
Newspaper
Diluted PVA (white) glue
Heavy corrugated cardboard
Strong clear glue
Masking tape
Fine sandpaper
White paint
Assortment of poster paints
Non-toxic clear gloss varnish

1 Coat the inside of the bowl with five layers of PVA-soaked newspaper strips, allowing for an overlap of 2½ cm (1 in). Leave to dry in a warm place for 48 hours.

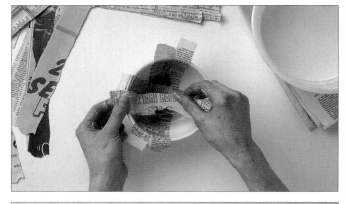

2 Gently prise the paper bowl from its mould with a blunt knife, and leave it upside down to dry for a few hours.

3 Trim the ragged edge to about ½ cm (¼ in).

4 Cut a zigzag bowl rim from the thick cardboard and lay it on the top of the papier-mâché bowl rim. Stick the rim on the bowl with strong clear glue, and hold it in place with masking tape. Allow the glue to dry for an hour or so and then paper over the rim, covering the joins carefully.

5 Paper the underside of the rim in the same way. Leave the bowl to dry for 24 hours. Lightly sand down the surface of the bowl, and then prime it with two coats of white paint.

6 Draw in any decoration with pencil first, and then decorate the bowl with poster paints. Let the bowl dry thoroughly, and then seal it with two coats of clear gloss varnish.

STAINED GLASS PENDANT

Hang this 'stained glass' pendant in your window and enjoy the bright colours as the light shines through. You could choose your own design from a plate or a piece of jewellery or you could base it on the Celtic ship used here.

YOU WILL NEED
Black cartridge paper
Craft knife
Coloured tissue paper
Glue
Ribbon

1 Trace and draw out your designs twice in black cartridge paper and then cut out the shapes with a sharp craft knife. Be careful to cut inside the lines so that the shape remains intact.

2 Select which colour tissue paper is to go where and trace off and cut to shape. Start to glue your tissue paper on to the back of one of the black frames, using a separate piece to cover each area. You can use as many or as few colours as you wish. When you feel more confident you can start to shade your picture by putting one layer of paper over another, giving a darker tone.

3 When all the shapes have been filled, glue and fix the other black frame on to the back to neaten. Attach a ribbon to the top and display in your window.

DECORATIVE ORNAMENTS AND GIFTS

ABSTRACT STAINED GLASS

This is a very effective but easy way to make an abstract piece of 'stained glass' work, which is great fun to do and because the pieces are torn it is always slightly unpredictable.

YOU WILL NEED
Two sheets of black paper
Coloured tissue paper
Glue

1 Cut out two identical frames from the sheets of black paper. Take the coloured tissue papers and tear them into strips.

2 Cut out two pieces of tissue paper just larger than the frame opening, one in a light colour and one in a darker colour. Glue the lighter one onto the back of one of the frames. Arrange the torn strips so that they overlap the edges of the lighter tissue paper, and glue them into place.

3 Finally, stick down the darker piece of tissue paper, sandwiching the strips in place. Glue down the other black frame on top.

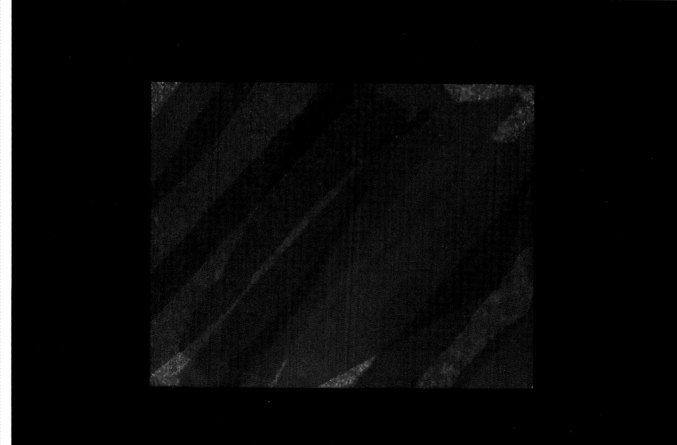

PLAQUE

Your family may have a coat of arms or a heraldic device that could be displayed on a wall plaque – if it hasn't, why not invent one? Add a Latin motto or phrase for authenticity – the wittier the better!

YOU WILL NEED
Thick cardboard
Strong clear glue
Masking tape
Diluted PVA (white) glue
2 picture hangers
Newspaper
Fine sandpaper
White paint
Selection of poster paints
Non-toxic clear gloss varnish
Chain or cord to hang plaque

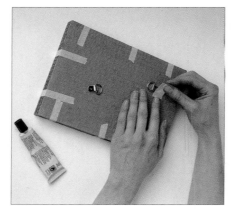

1 Cut three identical pieces of cardboard to the required dimensions, and stick them together with strong clear glue, securing the edges with masking tape. Paint the plaque with a coat of diluted PVA glue and allow it to dry. Stick two picture hangers to the reverse of the plaque with strong clear glue, and secure the stem of each hanger with a piece of masking tape.

2 Next, let the glue behind the hangers dry for at least an hour, and then cover the plaque with five layers of papier-mâché, using strips of newspaper approximately 2½ cm (1 in) wide, soaked in PVA glue.

3 Lightly sand down the surface of the plaque, and then apply two layers of white paint. Leave time for the paint to dry thoroughly.

4 Finally, draw in your design with pencil, and decorate the plaque with poster paints. Seal the finished plaque with two coats of non-toxic clear gloss varnish. Attach a chain or cord to the hangers on the reverse side to suspend it from the wall.

FRAMED PIECE

If you have a spare frame or a gap on a wall that you have been wondering how to fill, here is a way to make a charming abstract seashore scene. You can vary the images to make a series of pieces for different sized frames.

YOU WILL NEED
Stencilling card
Craft knife
Assortment of coloured papers
Glue

1 Scale up the design on the template to the size that you require for your frame. Draw it out onto a piece of stencilling card and carefully cut out the lines using a craft knife so that the shapes show through. Take care not to cut through any 'bridges' in the card.

2 Next, place the cut-out stencil onto the piece of coloured paper which will form the main background. Then cut out squares or rectangles of different coloured papers until you have enough to fill the spaces in the stencil design.

3 Arrange the coloured papers by placing them between the stencilling card and the background paper, and see how they give form to the shapes.

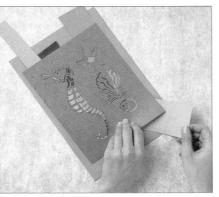

4 When you have decided on the colours for the final picture, glue all the pieces into position. Finally, trim the pieces of coloured paper that extend beyond the stencil and secure the picture into a frame.

Party Accessories and Festive Decorations

Everyone loves a party, and here you will find plenty of ideas
to impress your friends and family. There are projects for
decorative napkins, a delightful doily, colourful place mats
and name tags; there are suggestions for themed parties, such as
an Egyptian Evening – or why not join the Knights of the
Round Table with the Twelfth Knight party pieces? The festive
decorations include a pretty Easter Egg Basket, and a beautiful
Advent Calendar to count the days to Christmas.

WELL-DRESSED NAPKIN

Here is a quick and simple way to dress up a napkin using coloured card. You can make the holder in contrasting or a toning coloured card to suit the setting.

YOU WILL NEED
Paper napkins
Thin card (stock) in two contrasting
  colours
Glue

1 First cut a square of card to the same size as the folded napkin.

2 Fold the card diagonally with the front fold halfway up. Cut a triangle in contrasting coloured card slightly smaller than the front triangle. Cut out a zigzag edge along two sides.

3 Now fold the napkin in half and place it into the napkin holder. Why not experiment with different designs on the front, or leave it plain and glue on a cut out motif from a magazine.

SPOT-ON NAPKINS

This is a quick and bright way to decorate your paper napkins for children's parties or a special theme dinner. The basic idea is to split the layers of two different coloured napkins, then join them together and cut out shapes in one colour in order to reveal the other.

YOU WILL NEED
Two packets of contrasting coloured paper napkins
Glue

1 Take two paper napkins of different colours. Here a light and a dark colour are used. They should be the same size and preferably the same make so that they fit together exactly. Most napkins are three-ply (three layers). Start by splitting them so that you are working with two layers of each colour. The reason for this is so that the finished napkin is not too thick.

2 Fold the lighter coloured napkin diagonally and cut into two.

3 Carefully glue one half onto the darker napkin. Cut out light-coloured spots from the other half and glue them onto the dark triangle.

4 Now cut out spots from another dark napkin and glue these to the lighter triangle.

RING THE CHANGES

Using small pieces of coloured card you can create several different eye-catching napkin rings. Add contrasting coloured motifs, or simply cut and slot them into interesting shapes.

YOU WILL NEED
Coloured card (stock)
Contrasting coloured paper
Glue

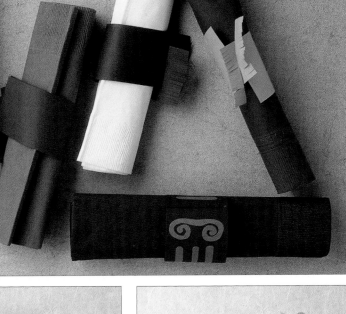

1 Take a plain band of card measuring 15 × 5 cm (6 × 2 in). For the classical column design cut out the 'capital' and 'flutes' from contrasting colour paper and stick them onto the plain strip.

2 When the strip has been decorated, dab some glue onto one end and bring the other end around to join. Hold the ends in place until the glue has dried.

3 For the blue napkin ring, shape the ends by drawing and cutting out a design, so that when the ends are brought together the band looks more interesting.

4 To finish off add a contrasting colour circle with a blue dot in the centre.

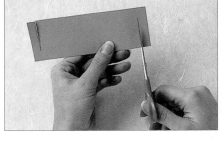

5 For the asymmetrical rings, take a strip the same size as before and cut a 4 cm (1¼ in) slot, 1 cm (³⁄₈ in) in from the end and parallel to it. Repeat the same on the other end but making sure that the slot is cut from the opposite edge.

6 Now cut the ends and interlink the slots so that they hold together. Decorate the ends by fringing or cutting triangles in them. By varying the size of the darts you can experiment with different effects.

80

DECORATIVE DOILY

A circle of lightweight coloured card in a contrasting colour forms a base for this tissue paper doily and sets it off to best effect. You can also use the techniques described here to create a unique design for greetings cards.

YOU WILL NEED
Lightweight card (stock)
Tissue paper
Glue

1 To get a good-sized doily, draw around a dinner plate and cut out two circles, one in card and the other in tissue paper.

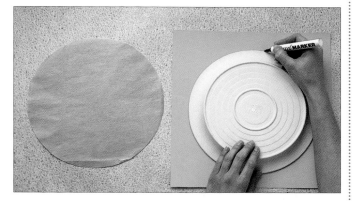

2 Fold the tissue paper in half three times to form an eighth and cut a scalloped pattern around the curved edge.

3 Fold it in half again and lightly draw a small geometric design along the edge and then cut these shapes out.

4 Unfold back to an eighth of the circle and fold the two edges of the segment to the centre. Draw and cut out your design as before on both edges. Unfold the doily and place on the card for a decorative effect.

PLACES ON A THEME

Simple ideas are often the most striking, and so here are some suggestions for place cards made using a collage technique, creating a theme for your table setting.

YOU WILL NEED
Two pieces of contrasting coloured card (stock) or paper
Glue
Gold metallic pen
Metallic crêpe paper

1 Draw and cut out a snail shape from coloured paper. Glue it onto the front of a contrasting place card. Use any animal image: you could even give each person an individual animal!

2 For a Mexican theme for your table setting, cut out a cactus shape in green paper or card and stick it onto a yellow place card. Draw on small dots with a gold pen to indicate the prickles.

3 To introduce a touch of frivolity to your table, make up this jolly bow-tie card. Take a rectangle of metallic crêpe paper and fold the ends to the middle. Glue ends in place. Take a smaller strip of crêpe paper and wrap around the centre of the bow to pull into shape. Glue ends in place.

4 Finally glue the bow-tie to the top of the place card.

STAND-UP PLACE NAMES

Make your place cards really stand out with these novelty motifs that project above the cards. Choose simple, recognizable shapes cut out from contrasting coloured card.

YOU WILL NEED
Green, orange, red and white card (stock)
Glue
Gold metallic pen
Craft knife

1 Take a square of green card and fold in half. Cut out an octopus shape from orange card but instead of gluing it directly onto the green card, position it so that the top half is above the fold line. Cut out the facial features from the green card and glue in place.

2 For a festive name place, cut out two holly leaves in green. Fix them onto the top of a red place card so that the holly is sticking upwards. Cut out and glue on red dots to make the berries.

3 To make this rocket name card, fold then unfold the name card and lay flat. Draw on the spaceship shape onto the lower half with gold pen so that the top of the rocket extends over the halfway line. With a craft knife, cut around the top part of the rocket only. Then fold the card in half again and the rocket will stand up.

TWELFTH KNIGHT

Whether entertaining the Knights of the Round Table or just arranging a boys' party, these heraldic place mats will certainly set the tone.

YOU WILL NEED
Silver, purple and orange card (stock)
Glue

2 Cut out eight wavy lines in orange card and five dots in purple card. Using the template, scaled to the size required, draw and cut out the fleur-de-lys shape.

1 Place mat
To make this heraldic place mat, trace out a shield shape onto silver card and cut it out. It should have a width and length of about 25 cm (10 in). Cut six strips of purple card measuring 2 × 27 cm (¾ × 11 in). Glue and place two strips to form a cross on the shield and trim at the edges.

3 Following the design in the photograph, arrange all the shapes onto your card and glue them into place one by one.

4 Napkin holder
Take a piece of purple card 22 × 5 cm (9 × 2 in). Join the short ends together and glue. Cut out a small silver shield in card and an orange fleur-de-lys. Glue together and then glue onto the napkin holder.

5 Name place card
To complete the heraldic theme, make up a name place. Cut a piece of silver card 9 × 10 cm (3½ × 4 in) and fold it lengthways down the centre. Cut out a smaller fleur-de-lys shape 4 cm (1½ in) high in purple card and glue it onto the silver card. Add the orange band.

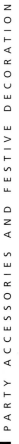

EGYPTIAN EVENING

Ancient Egypt is the inspiration for this
exotic place setting of place mat,
napkin holder and name card
embellished in bronze and gold.

YOU WILL NEED
Thin card (stock)
Bronze, black and blue paper
Glue
Gold metallic pen
Black felt-tip pen (optional)
Sticky tape

1 Place mat
■ In order to make
up this place mat,
cut out a piece of
card in the shape of
a Pharaoh's head
which should
measure 30 cm
(12 in) across the
bottom and have a
height of 27 cm
(11 in). Cover the
card in bronze
coloured paper and,
in the centre area,
very lightly mark out
the shape of the face
in pencil. Cut the
beard out of black
paper, glue in place,
and then make a
criss-cross design on
it with a gold pen.
Scale up to the size
required the
features of the face
from the template
and cut out of black
paper and glue into
position or use a
black felt-tip pen to
draw them in.

2 Cut strips of blue
■ paper 2 cm (¾ in)
wide for the
headdress
decoration and start
to glue them in
parallel lines onto
the bronze card. The
strips at the top of
the head are slightly
curved. Add blue
dots for the earrings.

3 Napkin holder
■ To make the
Egyptian napkin
holder, first cut out
an 18 cm (7 in)
square of card. Cover
one side in bronze
paper and the other
side in black paper.
Fold up one side not
quite half-way, with
the bronze side
inside, and add blue
strips, fanning them
out as shown. Trim
the strips level with
the edge of card. Cut
out an Egyptian eye
motif in bronze
paper and fix it onto
the front.

4 Name place card
■ Cut out two
triangles in card.
Cover one side in
black paper. Join
them at the top by
cutting off the top
corner and taping
them together at the
back. Cut out a
bronze motif, glue
on the front then
use a gold pen to
write on the names
required.

THIS LITTLE PIGGY

Great for children's parties or for a more adult gathering, this piggy place setting will bring oinks of delight! Choose bright pink, or a pale pink for a Miss Piggy.

YOU WILL NEED
Circular plate
Pink, green and blue card (stock)
Glue
Craft knife
Felt-tip pen

1 Place mat
▬ Using a plate as a template, mark and cut out a circle about 24 cm (10 in) in diameter in pink card, remembering to include two ear shapes.

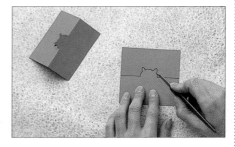

4 Name place card
▬ To make up the name card, take a piece of green card measuring 9 cm (3½ in) square. Draw a line down the centre and around the top half of the pig's head and ears. Score along the head and ears only and then gently fold, and the pig's head will stand up.

2 Using green and blue card, cut out and glue all the features of the face into position.

3 Then attach the curly tail to the right-hand side in order to give the finishing touch to your pig place mat.

5 Glue the piggy's features as before onto a piece of pink card and then attach the finished face on to the folded card. Add the curly tail.

6 Napkin holder
▬ Take a strip of pink card measuring 22 × 5 cm (8½ × 2 in) and glue the ends together. Before the glue has dried, slip a green curly tail card under the join and hold firmly until it is dry.

TIGER, TIGER

Dress up as a big cat with this colourful tiger mask that will set the scene for a jungle theme party.

YOU WILL NEED
Orange card (stock)
Black felt-tip pen
Black ribbon
Craft knife
Sticky tape
Sewing needle
Elastic

1 Use the template, scaled up to the size required, and cut out the tiger mask in some bright orange card.

2 Now draw on the tiger stripes with a black felt-tip pen.

3 For the whiskers cut thin strips of black ribbon about 12 × ½ cm (5 × ¼ in). Using a craft knife make four small slots on either side of the nose.

4 Push the whisker strips through the slots and use tape on the back to secure them.

5 Now sew on some elastic to either side of the mask and adjust to fit.

CONE HATS

With a simple change of decoration this basic cone hat can make a clown's hat or an elegant medieval headdress fit for a lady.

YOU WILL NEED
Card (stock)
Crêpe paper
Glue
Sticky tape

1 For the basic cone you will need to cut out a 60 cm (23 in) diameter semi-circle in card. You can make this measurement larger or smaller depending on the finished size you require. Roll the semi-circle into a cone and fasten with tape or glue.

2 To make the medieval cone cut streamers of crêpe paper in three different colours and push them through the end of the hat. Secure with sticky tape on the inside.

3 Now plait wider strips of the three colours of crêpe paper. Stick the plait onto the base of the cone.

4 To make the clown's hat make up pom-poms by cutting out three 20 cm (8 in) diameter circles of crêpe paper. Pinch each circle in the centre and twist. Now scrunch up the excess paper and mould it into a ball shape.

5 Push the first pom-pom through the top of the cone, then carefully make two slots one above the other down the front of the cone. Push the centre of the pom-poms through the slots and tape them on the inside to secure.

EASTER EGG BASKET

Make Easter eggs-tra special by giving this pretty gift-wrapped basket of eggs. Choose daffodil yellow card and tissue, or bright pink as here.

YOU WILL NEED
Old bowl-shaped container
Coloured card (stock)
Glue
Metallic tissue paper
Pink tissue paper
Pink ribbon
Chocolate eggs

1 Cut a strip of card large enough to go around the bowl and just a bit deeper. Then cut a wavy line along the top edge.

2 Glue the strip onto the bowl.

3 Now take a square of metallic tissue paper and place it in the bottom of the bowl.

4 Scrunch up a large sheet of bright pink tissue paper and arrange it in the bottom of the bowl. Place the chocolate eggs inside on the pink tissue paper. Bring the metallic tissue paper around and tie together with some pink ribbon.

ADVENT CALENDAR

Make the countdown to Christmas even more exciting with this beautiful tree Advent calendar. The windows are decorated with pictures cut out from old Christmas cards.

YOU WILL NEED
Red, green and orange card (stock)
Thin cardboard
Craft knife
Old greetings cards
Glue
Silver metallic pen

1 Cut out two tree shapes, one in red card and the other in green. Use a 2 cm (¾ in) square template of thin cardboard to mark out 25 windows at random on the green tree. Now cut along three sides of each window with a craft knife.

2 Place the green tree onto the red tree so that it is slightly higher and gives the green tree a red line on the bottom edges. Carefully open each window and mark their position on the red tree in pencil. Remove the green tree. Cut out 25 small pictures from old Christmas cards and glue them onto the pencilled squares on the red Christmas tree.

3 Now glue the green tree onto the red one making sure that all the windows line up.

4 Decorate the tree with cut-out circles of red and orange card to suggest the Christmas tree baubles.

5 Using a silver pen draw a bow above each bauble and then number the windows 1 to 25.

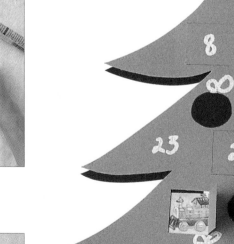

IT'S A CRACKER

Everyone loves to pull crackers at Christmas. It is also a fun way to disguise the shape of a gift by dressing it up as a cracker. You can also use them as decorations for your tree.

YOU WILL NEED
Cardboard tube
Wrapping paper
Double-sided tape
Ribbon

1 Place your gift inside the cardboard tube and cut a piece of wrapping paper so that it extends about 10 cm (4 in) at either end. Roll the paper around and secure it with tape. For a really professional look double-sided tape should be used.

2 Now cut two lengths of ribbon and tie at each end of the tube. Trim the ribbon ends. For a more colourful effect you could use several colours of ribbon.

3 Holding the cracker in one hand, cut a zigzag design at the end and then turn around and repeat with the other end.

3-D CHRISTMAS TREE

Make a paper Christmas tree stand out by adding extra layers. Smother it with self-adhesive stars for a quick and easy decorative touch.

YOU WILL NEED
Coloured card (stock) in three colours
Glue
Self-adhesive stars
Ribbon

1 Cut out three Christmas tree shapes, in three different colours, so that they are gradually smaller in size.

2 Now cut twelve small squares of card and glue six of them together one on top of the other to make a block. Glue the other six in the same way. Glue one card block onto the top of the largest tree and the second one onto the middle-sized tree.

3 Glue the tip of the middle-sized tree onto the largest tree and the smallest tree onto the top of the middle-sized tree.

4 Now decorate all three trees with sticky stars. Attach a ribbon at the back so that it can be hung up to be displayed.

Dress up your tree with shimmering bows for a glamorous film-star style Christmas. Match bows to baubles for a co-ordinated look.

YOU WILL NEED
Metallic corrugated paper
Stapler
Metallic tissue paper
Double-sided tape
Ribbon

1 From the metallic corrugated paper cut out an oblong measuring 18 × 12 cm (7 × 4½ in). Gather in the centre to make the bow shape and staple in position.

2 Now take a length of metallic tissue paper and wrap it around the centre of the bow to cover the staples. However do not wrap the whole length around but leave some excess to fall at the front. Fix at the back with double-sided tape.

3 Now cut two rectangles for the tails in the metallic paper measuring 20 × 8 cm (8 × 3 in). Cut darts at one end of each tail.

4 Make one pleat at the top of the tails. Staple each pleat and then staple the tails together.

5 Now attach the tails to the back of the bow with double-sided tape. Make a loop with a piece of ribbon and stick it to the back of the finished bow for hanging.

CHRISTMAS TREE
GIFT BOX

Here is a way to make a very attractive Christmas decoration to hang on the tree. Pop a chocolate or small gift inside or leave it empty simply for decoration.

YOU WILL NEED
White card (stock)
Craft knife
Ruler
Glue
Wrapping paper
Ribbon

1 Using the template, scaled to the size required, draw and cut out the box shape in white card.

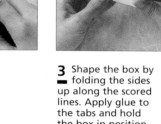

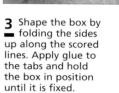

2 Score along all the lines using a craft knife and ruler, taking care not to cut through the card completely.

3 Shape the box by folding the sides up along the scored lines. Apply glue to the tabs and hold the box in position until it is fixed.

4 Now cover the box in an appropriate wrapping paper.

5 Finish off by tying a ribbon decoratively, and making a loop to hang the box on the tree.

INDEX

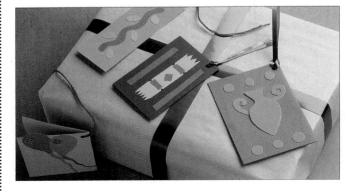